BIKING

By S.L. Hamilton

VISIT US AT
WWW.ABDOPUBLISHING.COM

Published by ABDO Publishing Company, 8000 West 78th Street, Suite 310, Edina, MN 55439. Copyright ©2010 by Abdo Consulting Group, Inc. International copyrights reserved in all countries. No part of this book may be reproduced in any form without written permission from the publisher. A&D Xtreme™ is a trademark and logo of ABDO Publishing Company.

Printed in the United States of America, North Mankato, Minnesota.
102009
012010

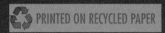 PRINTED ON RECYCLED PAPER

Editor: John Hamilton
Graphic Design: Sue Hamilton
Cover Design: John Hamilton
Cover Photo: Getty Images
Interior Photos: AP-pgs 6, 7, 10, 11, 14, 15, 20, 21, 24, 25, & 29; Corbis-pgs 16, 17, 26, & 27; Getty Images-pgs 1, 2, 3, 4, 5, 8, 9, 12, 13, 18, 19, 22, 23, 28, 30, 31, & 32; Jupiterimages-pg 16; and Race Across America-pg 27.

Library of Congress Cataloging-in-Publication Data

Hamilton, S.L., 1959-
   Biking / S.L. Hamilton.
      p. cm. -- (Xtreme sports)
   Includes index.
   ISBN 978-1-61613-002-2
   1. Cycling--Juvenile literature. I. Title.
   GV1043.5.H36 2010
   796.6--dc22
                              2009034938

CONTENTS

XTREME

X̌treme Quote   "Get a bicycle. You will not regret it if you live."   ~Mark Twain

BIKING

Extreme bikers may take on life-threatening mountain trails, bone-shattering dirt tracks, or body-breaking marathons.

BMX

"BMX" stands for bicycle motocross. (Motocross is an off-road motorcycle race.) "X" is a symbol for "cross." BMX biking began in California in the 1960s. Kids raced their bikes, instead of motorcycles, on motocross-type dirt tracks.

BIKING

X̶treme Quote

"Most likely you'd leave with a story
to tell and a concussion."
~Dennis McCoy on early BMX races

BMX Racing

BMX racers ride on a BMX track that is 985-1,300 feet (300-396 m) in length. Up to eight riders compete in a race, or "heat," at one time. Several preliminary heats are run, with the winners qualifying to compete in the final. The winner of the final is the winner of the event.

"If you want to experience all of the successes and pleasures in life, you have to be willing to accept all the pain and failure that comes with it." ~Mat Hoffman, BMX Rider

BMX Freestyle: Ramp & Dirt Jumping

Freestyle BMXers use their bikes to perform super-high jumps and unique stunts. Dirt jumping sends the riders up high, where they perform gravity-defying tricks.

Xtreme Moves

A barspin allows the bike's handlebars to spin completely around. A tailwhip allows the bike to spin independent of the handlebars.

BMX Freestyle: Flatland

Flatland BMXing keeps the bike mostly on a smooth, flat surface. A rider needs intense balance and coordination to stand or spin the bike. Special front and back pegs are attached at the bike's axles, providing a foot or handhold for the flatlander.

Pegs

13

BMX: An Olympic Sport

Bicycle motocross became an Olympic event for the first time during the 2008 Summer Olympic Games held in Beijing, China. The sport drew BMXers from around the world. The countries of Latvia (men's) and France (women's) brought home gold medals.

U.S. BMXers Mike Day (#365) and Donny Robinson (#10) won silver and bronze medals in the 2008 Olympics.

MOUNTAIN

Mountain biking takes riders off-roading. Dangers are everywhere. From sharp, loose rocks, to trees, to raging streams, mountain bikers travel to the extreme.

BIKING

The Bike

Mountain bikers take on the most rugged conditions they can find. There are five different mountain bike types: cross country, trail, downhill, freeride, and dirt jump. Although each is specially designed for unique terrain, all mountain bikes are built with an extra-sturdy suspension and stronger brakes.

Slickrock Bike Trail

Slickrock Bike Trail is one of the most famous mountain bike trails in the world. It is located near Moab, Utah. In the Old West, metal horseshoes often slipped on the "slick rock." The wheels of modern mountain bike "stick" to the gritty sandstone trail. The trail is marked with paint, so riders have a path to follow.

Xtreme Quote

"If you're riding a cheap bike, check the fillings in your teeth."
~Utah Mountain Biking on Slickrock's Difficulty

ICE

BIKING

Ice biking is also called snow biking. Riders use heavy-duty mountain bikes equipped with studded tires. Powerful leg muscles are needed to plow through heavy snow, but riders enjoy creating the first new trail.

ROAD

The most famous road race is France's Tour de France, which is held each summer. It is a "stage race," with different sections of roads raced each day for three weeks.

Xtreme Fact

American Lance Armstrong is one of the most well-known road racers.

24

RACING

Lance
Armstrong

25

Ultra Marathon

An ultra marathon is a long, grueling race. For days, ultracyclists pedal as fast and far as they can, stopping only when they can't continue. The first to cross the finish line wins. A well-known ultra marathon is Race Across America (RAAM). It goes from coast-to-coast, covering more than 3,000 miles (4,828 km).

BIKE

Lance Armstrong wears a special aerodynamic racing helmet for the Tour de France.

Bike helmets vary depending on the cyclist's needs, but serious riders always wear helmets.

HELMETS

High-risk biking, such as downhill or mountain riding, requires the extra protection found in a full-face helmet.

treme Quote

"What do you call a cyclist who doesn't wear a helmet? An organ donor." ~David Perry

THE

Concussion
A severe blow to the head that injures the brain and may cause confusion or a temporary loss of consciousness.

Final
The last race that determines the ultimate winner of a contest.

Heat
A preliminary race where the winner goes on to compete in additional heats, until the last contest, or final, determines the race's winner.

Lance Armstrong
Award-winning athlete and seven-time winner of the Tour de France road race from 1999 to 2005. A cancer survivor, Armstrong works to support cancer research through the Lance Armstrong Foundation.

define the sport of Freestyle BMX. Nicknamed "The Condor," he is considered one of the best vertical ramp riders in the history of the sport.

Motocross
A motorcycle or all-terrain vehicle race held on an off-road dirt track. Bicycle racers use the same type of dirt tracks to run non-motorized races.

Stunt
An activity that requires specific physical skills, strength, and daring.

Suspension
Parts of a bike that "suspend" the rider and provide protection from the terrain over which he or she is traveling.

INDEX